What's Inside Me?
My Bones and Muscles

¿Qué hay dentro de mí?
Huesos y músculos

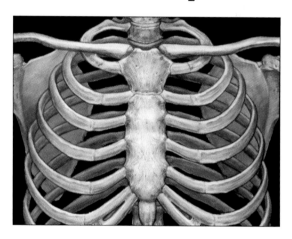

Dana Meachen Rau

Marshall Cavendish
Benchmark
New York

My Bones

Huesos

SKULL
CRÁNEO

RIB CAGE
CAJA TORÁXICA

BACKBONE
COLUMNA
VERTEBRAL

PELVIS

JOINTS
ARTICULACIONES

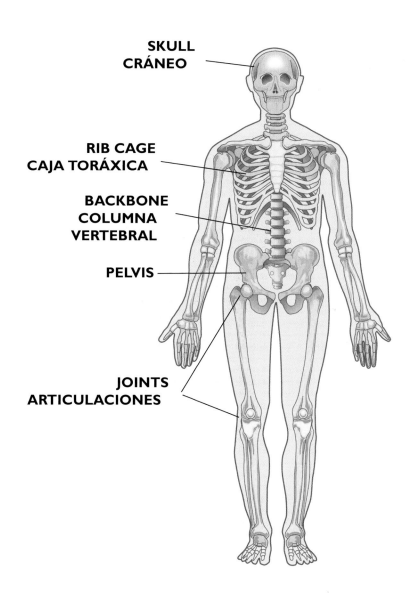

Stand still. Bend over. Wave your arms.
Kick your legs.

❖

Quédate quieto. Agáchate. Agita los
brazos. Patea.

Your bones and your muscles help your
body do all of these things.

❖

Los huesos y músculos ayudan a tu cuerpo
a hacer todas estas cosas.

Have you ever seen a house being built? First, it needs a *framework*. This keeps the house standing.

Your bones are the framework for your body. Without bones, your skin and inside parts would fall to the floor.

❖

¿Haz visto alguna vez la construcción de una casa? Primero, se necesita un *armazón* para mantener la casa en pie.

Los huesos son el armazón de tu cuerpo. Sin los huesos, tu piel y los órganos internos se caerían al suelo.

You have 206 bones in your body. All your bones together are called your *skeleton*.

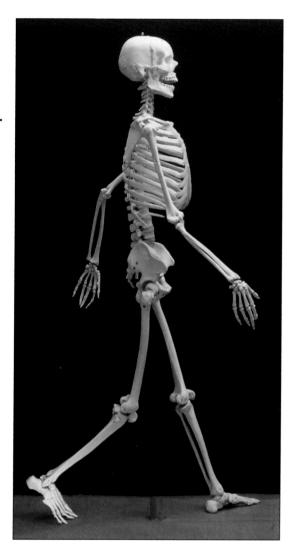

Hay 206 huesos en el cuerpo humano. El conjunto de los huesos se llama *esqueleto*.

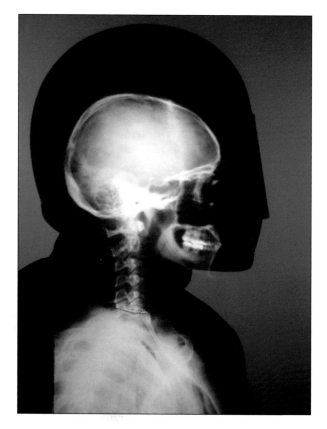

You can see your skeleton with an *X-ray*.

Puedes ver el esqueleto con los *rayos X*.

Look closely at a bone. The outside is hard. The inside is soft and filled with tiny holes.

❖

Mira un hueso de cerca. El exterior es duro. El interior es suave y lleno de pequeños huecos.

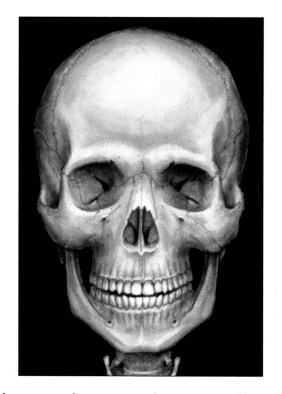

Your *skull* is made up of many flat bones.
Your skull protects your brain.

El *cráneo* está formado por muchos huesos
planos. El cráneo protege tu cerebro.

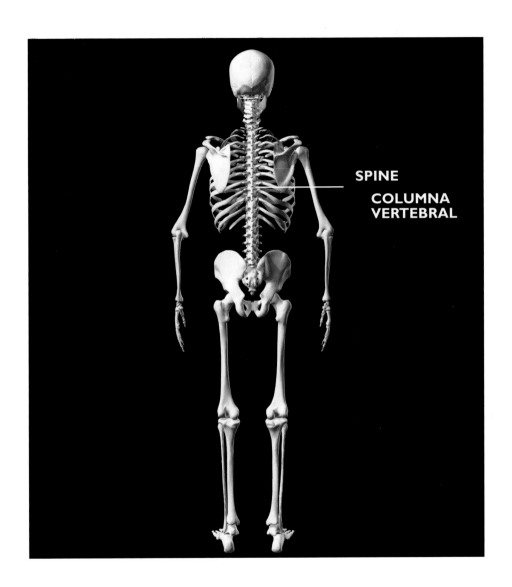

SPINE

COLUMNA VERTEBRAL

The small round bones down your back make up your *spine*. Your spine helps you stand straight.

You have long bones in your arms and legs. You have tiny bones in your hands and feet.

Los pequeños huesos redondos en tu espalda forman la *columna vertebral*. La columna vertebral te ayuda a pararte derecho.

Tienes huesos largos en los brazos y piernas. Tienes huesos pequeños en las manos y pies.

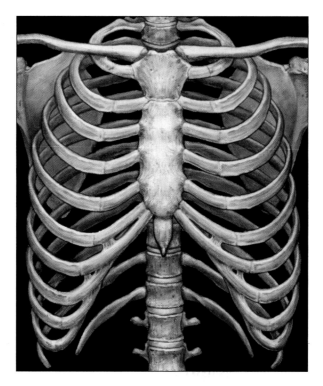

Your *rib cage* is made up of the curved bones in your chest. It protects your heart and lungs.

❖

La *caja toráxica* en tu pecho tiene huesos curvos que protegen el corazón y los pulmones.

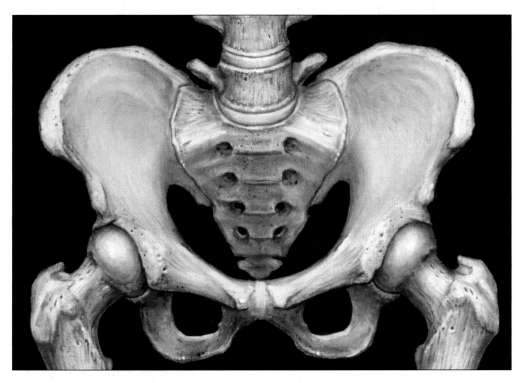

Your *pelvis* is a large, flat bone. It helps hold up your body.

❖

La *pelvis* es un hueso grande y plano que sostiene el cuerpo.

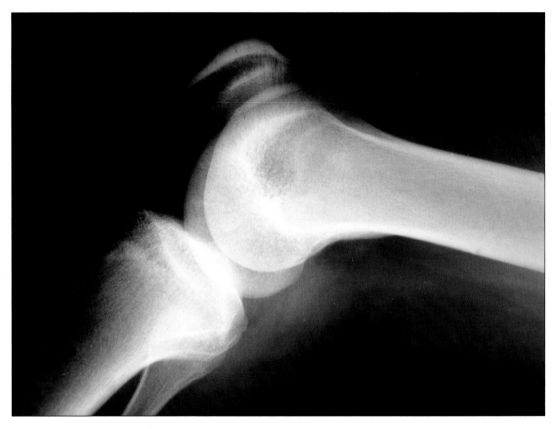

X-ray of a knee joint

❖

Rayos X de la articulación de la rodilla

A *joint* is where two bones meet. *Ligaments* connect these bones to each other.

Joints in your elbows and knees move in one direction. Joints in your shoulders and wrists move around in a circle.

Una *articulación* es donde dos huesos se encuentran. Los *ligamentos* unen estos huesos entre sí.

Las articulaciones de los codos y las rodillas se mueven en una dirección. Las articulaciones de los hombros y las muñecas se mueven en círculo.

Bones cannot move without muscles. Most muscles are red and striped.

There are more than 600 muscles in your body.

Los huesos no pueden moverse sin los músculos. La mayoría de los músculos son fibras rojas.

Hay más de 600 músculos en el cuerpo.

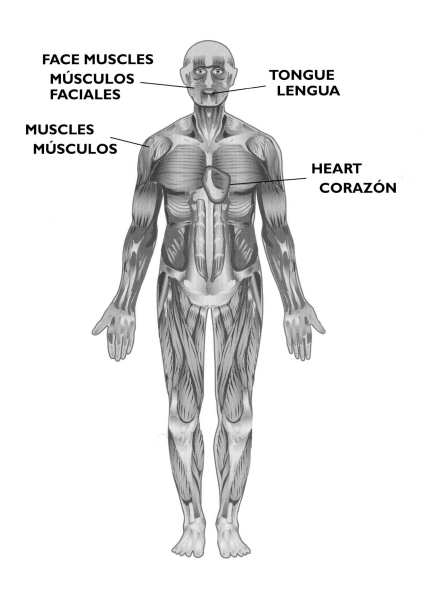

FACE MUSCLES
MÚSCULOS
FACIALES

TONGUE
LENGUA

MUSCLES
MÚSCULOS

HEART
CORAZÓN

19

Your hand muscles help you write a letter.
You use your leg and foot muscles when you
walk or run.

❖

Los músculos de la mano te ayudan a escribir
una carta. Cuando caminas o corres usas los
músculos de los pies y de las piernas.

Every time you move, your muscles are at work.

❖

Cuando te mueves, los músculos están trabajando.

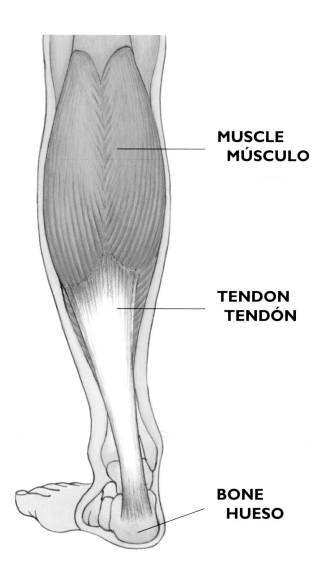

MUSCLE
MÚSCULO

TENDON
TENDÓN

BONE
HUESO

Strong cords called *tendons* attach muscles to bones. When a muscle moves, it pulls the bone.

That is how you can raise your hand or point with your finger.

Los cordones fuertes que conectan los músculos a los huesos se llaman *tendones*. Cuando un músculo se mueve, tira del hueso.

Así es como puedes levantar la mano o señalar con el dedo.

Muscles in your face move your eyebrows, mouth, and cheeks to make you look sad, happy, or angry. You use about 17 face muscles when you smile.

———————❖———————

Los músculos de la cara mueven las cejas, la boca y las mejillas para que te veas triste, feliz o enojado. Cuando sonríes, usas alrededor de 17 músculos faciales.

Some muscles have other jobs, too. Your tongue is a muscle. It helps you swallow food.

❖

Algunos músculos también tienen otras tareas. La lengua es un músculo que te ayuda a tragar la comida.

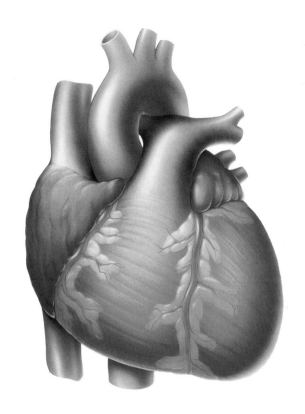

Your heart is a muscle. It pumps blood around your body.

❖

El corazón es un músculo que bombea sangre por todo el cuerpo.

Your body needs exercise. Get out of your chair and take a walk with a friend. It will keep your bones and muscles strong.

Tu cuerpo necesita ejercicio. Deja tu silla y sal a caminar con amigos para mantener fuertes tus huesos y músculos.

Challenge Words

framework The stiff inside parts that keep something standing up.

joint Where two bones meet.

ligaments Bands of body tissue that connect one bone to another.

pelvis A large, flat bone in your hips.

rib cage The curved bones in your chest.

skeleton All of your bones.

skull The bones in your head.

spine The line of small bones running down your back.

tendons Strong cords that attach muscles to bones.

X-ray A picture of your bones.

Palabras avanzadas

armazón Las partes internas fuertes que mantienen algo parado.

articulación Donde dos huesos se encuentran.

caja toráxica Los huesos curvos del pecho.

columna vertebral La hilera de huesos pequeños que baja por la espalda.

cráneo Los huesos de la cabeza.

esqueleto Todos los huesos del cuerpo.

ligamentos Las bandas de tejido que conectan un hueso con otro.

pelvis Un hueso grande y plano en las caderas.

rayos X Las fotografías de los huesos.

tendones Los cordones fuertes que unen los músculos a los huesos.

Index

Índice

With thanks to Nanci Vargus, Ed.D.
and Beth Walker Gambro, reading consultants

Marshall Cavendish Benchmark
99 White Plains Road
Tarrytown, New York 10591-9001
www.marshallcavendish.us

Library of Congress Cataloging-in-Publication Data

Rau, Dana Meachen, 1971–
[My bones and muscles. Spanish & English]
My bones and muscles = Huesos y músculos / by Dana Meachen Rau. — Bilingual ed.
p. cm. — (Bookworms. What's inside me?/¿Qué hay dentro de mí?)
Includes bibliographical references and index.
ISBN-13: 978-0-7614-2479-6 (bilingual edition : alk. paper)
ISBN-10: 0-7614-2479-2 (bilingual edition : alk. paper)
ISBN-13: 978-0-7614-2401-7 (Spanish edition : alk. paper)
ISBN-10: 0-7614-1777-X (English edition : alk. paper)
1. Musculoskeletal system—Juvenile literature. I. Title. II. Title: Huesos y músculos. III. Series:
Rau, Dana Meachen, 1971– Bookworms. What's inside me? (Spanish & English)

QM100.R3818 2006b
612.7—dc22
2006016553

Spanish Translation and Text Composition by Victory Productions, Inc.
www.victoryprd.com

Photo Research by Anne Burns Image

Cover Photo by Corbis/Royalty Free

The photographs in this book are published with the permission and through the courtesy of:
Peter Arnold: pp. 1, 11, 14, 15 Alex Grey; p. 8 Manfred Kage; p. 9 James V. Elmore; pp. 10, 16 Ed Reschke.
Jay Mallin: p. 2. Corbis: p. 5 Franco Vogt; p. 6 Joseph Sohm; pp. 4, 20 LWA-Dann Tardif; p. 21 Norbert Schaefer;
p. 25 Tom & Dee Ann McCarthy; pp. 26 Torleif Svensson; p. 28 Royalty Free.
Photo Researchers: p. 12 Roger Harris; p. 27 Brian Evans. Custom Medical Stock Photo: p. 22.

Series design by Becky Terhune
Illustrations by Ian Warpole

Printed in Malaysia
1 3 5 6 4 2